shout
annual 2012

shout *annual 201*

mates Is your friendship forever?

dates Hollywood V. Real Life!

lookin' great The *ultimate* A-Z of fashion & beauty

+ HOT BOYS... QUIZZES... HOROSCOPES... TRUE STORIES... CELEBS

what's inside?

page **19**

page **27**

page **79**

page **88**

page 33

page 62

page 10

Visit our fabulous website at
www.shoutmag.co.uk
for 24/7 shout fun!

Fashion FIXER!

The quiz that makes those tricky wardrobe decisions for you!

1 WHAT HAVE YOU GOT PLANNED FOR THE DAY?

- Nothing yet, so you need to be prepared for anything!
- Hanging out with your mates — and there's a chance you'll see your crush!
- You're heading to a party later, so you need an outfit for that!
- Spending time with your family — but you might escape later on!

2 WHOSE STYLE DO YOU MOST ADMIRE?

- Katy Perry.
- Kim Kardashian.
- Frankie from The Saturdays.
- Taylor Momsen.

3 WHICH DESCRIPTION BEST SUITS YOUR STYLE?

- On-trend, but laid-back.
- Quirky and colourful.
- Glam and girlie.
- Rock-chick cool.

4 IF YOU WENT ON A MAJOR SHOPPING SPREE, THE FIRST THING YOU'D BUY IS...

- Some mega-high heels — you can never have too many shoes!
- A leather jacket — to rock up any outfit!
- Skinny jeans — they'll never go out of fashion!
- A cute polka-dot dress — girlie and retro is so you!

5 YOUR PARENTS THINK YOUR STYLE IS...

- Too grown-up.
- Scruffy.
- Simple.
- A bit strange sometimes.

6 YOUR DREAM DATE IS...

- Zac Efron.
- Justin Bieber.
- Russell Brand.
- R-Pattz.

Dress, Boohoo.com.

Shoes, Matalan.

Belt, ASOS.

Cardigan, ASOS.

Jeans, Internacionale.

Shoes, Matalan.

Skirt, George at Asda.

Top, Matalan.

Boots, Internacionale.

Cardigan, A|wear.

Playsuit, F&F at Tesco.

Shoes, Internacionale.

embarrassing
MOMENTS!
The only place that's safe for you to share your cringiest confessions!

Illustration by Mandy Dixon

£20 WINNER

"My jacket looked disgusting!"

"I was hanging out in Burger King with my mates one Saturday, and was super-excited when I spotted my crush walking through the door! He waved and sat down, but I noticed he was watching us.

"I was in a bit of a daze, thinking about my crush, so when my friend suddenly shouted my name, I got a huge fright! All my mates burst out laughing, and started pointing at my new white faux-fur jacket — it was covered in ketchup!

"I forgot I was holding a sachet of it in my hand and I must have squeezed it when they made me jump!

"My jacket looked disgusting, and I even spotted my crush having a good laugh at me, too — nightmare!"

Leah, Gloucester

CRINGE RATING

MAJORLY MORTIFYING! 👀👀👀   **KINDA CRINGEY!** 👀👀   **BARELY BLUSH-WORTHY!** 👀

Doggy Disaster!

"My crush had finally asked me if I wanted to hang out with him one weekend and I couldn't believe my luck! We decided to just take a walk in the park, so I decided to take my dog along, too.

"The date was going so well, and after about half an hour, we decided to sit down for a bit on a bench. Just as my crush began to lean in for a kiss, he suddenly jumped up and shouted, 'Yuck!' — my dog had peed on his leg!

"To be honest, I was actually quite relieved it wasn't something to do with me that had put him off, but I was still mortified! My crush's jeans were soaking, so he had to leave… and he hasn't been in touch since!"

Skye, Manchester

How Nude!

"I'd arranged to meet my bezzie at the swimming pool, but was running late. I rang her and said just to start getting changed, and I'd see her in there.

"When I finally arrived, I rushed straight to the changing rooms and called out my bezzie's name. As I headed further in, I came face-to-face with not one, but three naked men — I was in the wrong changing room!

"They looked as embarrassed as me, so no-one said a word as I turned and ran straight out again! When I found my mate, she thought it was totally hilarious, but I was so worried that I'd see the men again in the pool that I went home! Arrrgh!"

Libby, Perth 😳😳😳

Spew Okay?!

"It was my first day at a new school, and I had to get the bus, which I wasn't used to as I could walk to my old school.

"The first bit of my journey was fine, and I'd even started chatting to a couple of girls and a cute boy!

"As we turned a sharp corner, though, I started to feel really sick. I tried to stop talking and just concentrate on not throwing up, but the boy asked me if I was okay.

"I quickly opened my mouth to answer him, and spewed all down his top! The whole bus started complaining of the smell, and even the driver shouted to open the windows!

"Surprisingly, the boy was really sweet about it and said not to worry — it was still mortifying, though!"

Sara, Ipswich 😳😳😳

Shop Shame!

"I was shopping in town by myself, on the lookout for a dress to wear to a really important party, so I spent ages trying on different styles.

"I finally found one that looked great on me, but when it came to taking it off, it got stuck on my head! I'd half pulled it over, so it was totally covering my face and I couldn't see a thing!

"After shouting for help for about ten minutes, I realised no one was coming, and had to carefully edge out on to the shop floor to get an assistant!

"I still couldn't see anything, but could tell people were sniggering! Eventually, a girl took me back to the fitting rooms and helped me get it off. It was totally the most embarrassing moment of my life!"

Molly, Essex

Hobble Humiliation!

"I'd stupidly worn some really high, uncomfortable shoes to school one day, and by 11am, my feet were agony!

"My teacher sent me on an errand, right to the other end of the corridor, so I did my best to hobble along. As I got halfway, I couldn't bear it any longer and starting saying 'Ouch!' with every step — it seemed to help somehow!

"The corridor was dead, so I knew no one could hear me. Or so I thought… Suddenly, a door opened, and a teacher popped her head out to ask what all the noise was!

"When I explained, she insisted I go back into the class with her to get a plaster, which she put on my foot in front of about 20 sixth-formers! Cringe!"

Nadine, Woking 😳😳

Four Friends

EVERY GIRL SHOULD HAVE!

Forget having hundreds of fake friends — these girlies are all you need!

Imagine the convos this group of mates have!

The Flirt…
like Katy Perry!

WHY SHE'S A GREAT MATE…

She might be married now — but that doesn't stop Katy from being a full-blown flirt! Just check her out cosying up to Justin Bieber! And we all know that the best thing about flirty friends is that they always bring fit lads (plus friends!)… and we're sure you'll benefit from that. Flutter flutter!

BE MORE LIKE HER…

You heard how Katy won Russell's heart by throwing a bottle at his head, right? Take a leaf outta her book and don't get so hung up about making your crush your 'official' boyfriend already — just have a laugh! Try out all your best jokes… and your flirting technique will be top notch in no time!

With flirty friends come fit lads, score!

The Listener…
like Taylor Swift!

WHY SHE'S A GREAT MATE…

Got more steam to let off than a, uh, steam room? Then Taylor is your woman! She's been through a few tough times herself (this is the girl who was dumped in a 27-second phone call, y'know!) so she'll have loads of awesome advice… we bet she could even give our Laura a run for her money!

BE MORE LIKE HER…

Well, the most important thing is to actually listen to what she's saying! There's no point oohing and aahing and acting all sympathetic if you don't actually have a clue what she's on about… because you're too busy daydreaming about your own drama! Give her the ear-time she needs.

The Tomboy...
like Fergie!

WHY SHE'S A GREAT MATE...

Well, you're not going to impress your crush if the only thing you know about footballers is that Cheryl Cole used to be married to one, are ya?

The fabulous Fergie is used to hanging about with a bunch of boys in the Black Eyed Peas — so she must be as cool as a cucumber around 'em!

BE MORE LIKE HER...

Stop treating lads like they've just been beamed down by a UFO and realise that they have the same stresses as you!

We know they burp and belch and tell really baaad jokes a lot of the time... but they're also freaking out about failing their exams and never finding a gf. Sounds familiar, right?

Give your mates a night to remember and arrange a girls' night in!

The Party Animal...
like Rihanna!

WHY SHE'S A GREAT MATE...

This laydee is a proper party animal — hear her roar! She's always got the hottest ticket in town and you're guaranteed a great night when she's around...

RiRi is so rated that Katy Perry even got her to organise her hen party for her!

BE MORE LIKE HER...

Don't wait for someone else to sort out your Saturday night — do it yourself! We've all sat on the sofa at the weekend and whinged that we've got nowt to do... but you could totally cobble together a cool night if you wanted to!

Most peeps just need a lil' push and a shove — so make that YOUR job!

ARE YOU A
Style
Superstar?

See if you get full marks for fashion!

START

You can name four fashion designers.

NO

YES

Gaga's style is ground-breaking!

NO

NO

Fashion is so confusing!

YES

YES

Style is more important than comfort.

You wardrobe is full of basics.

NO

You ♥ The Saturdays' style!

NO

You like to stand out from the crowd.

NO

YES

NO

YES

NO

YES

Gok Wan scares you!

NO

You experiment with fashion!

YES

You live in jeans.

YES

YES

NO

YES

NO

YES

NO

Fashion Fail!

Uh-oh! Looks like you need to check out shout's fashion pages pronto! There's nothing wrong with being a bit behind the times, but fashion can be fun too, ya know!

So-so Stylista!

You like fashion, but you don't feel you have to follow every trend out there — that's a good attitude to have, missy! As long as you stay true to yourself, you'll look good!

Total Trend-setter!

Whoa! Lady Gaga could take some fashion tips from you! You're ahead of the pack when it comes to trends — just be careful you don't become a slave to fashion!

13

"A KIDNEY TRANSPLANT SAVED MY LIFE"

SARAH OWES EVERYTHING TO HER BRAVE SISTER...

When Sarah was 14, she was struck down with renal failure, which caused her kidneys to stop functioning properly and resulted in her being placed on dialysis — a medical procedure that takes over the role of the kidneys in a patient.

Sarah's outlook was bleak — without a kidney transplant, she had no chance of recovery. After being on the transplant waiting list for two years without a suitable donor being found, Sarah's sister Becca, who had just turned 18, was tested as a possible match.

"I COULDN'T BELIEVE SHE'D DO SOMETHING LIKE THAT FOR ME!"

Their family were delighted to find out that Becca was a suitable donor for Sarah and the two girls underwent gruelling operations — Becca's to remove a healthy kidney, and Sarah's to have the organ transplanted in to her body.

"The symptoms of my kidney failure started when I was 12," Sarah says. "I hadn't been feeling well for a few days when I was sent home from school. I was really confused and disorientated — one of my teachers even thought I was drunk! I was sick, and even though I was drinking loads to help keep my fluids up, I didn't need to go to the toilet.

"Later that night, I collapsed and was rushed to hospital! The doctors took blood and urine samples and realised something wasn't right. I was sent for a kidney biopsy — where a needle is placed under the skin to take tissue out for testing — so that I could be checked for any disease.

"I COLLAPSED AND WAS RUSHED TO HOSPITAL!"

"It was really unpleasant, but worse was yet to come — I found out I needed a transplant!

"There wasn't a kidney available, and no-one knew how long it would take to match me with a donor, so I was put on dialysis, which performed my kidney function for me, which included removing waste from my blood and any extra water from my body.

"It was really tiring travelling to hospital to have dialysis three times a week, and it meant that I missed out on a lot of school work and I was so tired that sometimes I wasn't able to do all the things I used to do

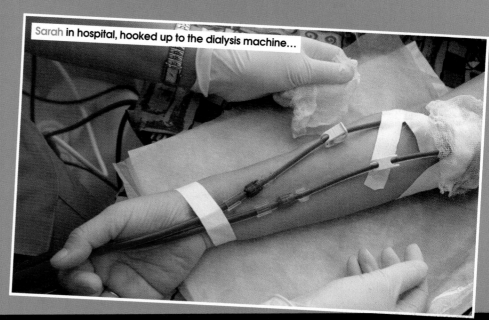
Sarah in hospital, hooked up to the dialysis machine...

including simple things like hanging out with my friends.

"After I'd been on the transplant list for a year-and-a-half, my transplant co-ordinator, who I'd been in touch with since my kidneys failed, arranged for me to have a meeting with her and the rest of my family. I remember thinking that this was strange as I'd only ever met my transplant co-ordinator with my mum.

"I WAS SO EMOTIONAL ABOUT EVERYTHING THAT WAS GOING ON..."

"When we got there, the co-ordinator talked to me about the option of using a live donor transplant — which would be a way of me getting a transplant without having to wait for someone to pass away.

"My mum and dad had already been tested, but they weren't a suitable match, but Becca decided that she wanted to get tested to see if she was a match! I was shocked at first. I was so overwhelmed that I burst into tears — I couldn't believe she'd do something like that for me!

"Over the next few weeks, we both underwent tests to see if our tissue types were a match, and when we were told that we'd be able to go ahead with the transplant, I was over the moon! I was so nervous that we wouldn't be a match, that when we found out the good news, it was like a massive weight was lifted off my shoulders! Finally, it looked like I could get back to living a normal life!

"On the day of the transplant, we were prepared for surgery. I kissed and hugged Becca goodbye as she

headed off for her operation — I was crying, but she seemed totally fine and even told me to stop being a wimp. I was so emotional about everything that was going on, I was still amazed that I was getting the operation, but I was also worried about both of our operations.

"Once Becca's kidney was removed successfully, I went down to the operating theatre to have it transplanted in to me. I was quite scared about getting the operation, but I was just so desperate to move on with my life that there was no way that I couldn't go through with it.

"When I came round from the operation, I was so weak and I remember feeling in pain, but when I turned to see Becca lying in the bed next to me, we just smiled at each other and I whispered "Thank you". Seeing Becca lying beside me made me feel so calm and relaxed, knowing that we were there for each other.

"My recovery from the operation was fairly quick — surprisingly, the donor has a much longer recovery period and Becca was pretty weak for about 12 weeks. It was hard for me to see her like this, because of me, but she told me to stop being stupid and that she knows that I would've done it for her.

"Now, we're both back to normal and are fighting fit, but I will always remember that I owe everything to my sister..."

BECCA SAYS:
"It was horrible seeing Sarah go through what she did. I would have done anything I could to help — and I'm just glad my kidney was a match and that the operation was a success!"

BIEBER FEVER!

Are Justin's fans, like, the craziest fans ever?

IVE GOT A BAD CASE OF BIEBER FEVER

BELIEBERS CAUSE CHAOS!

■ When touring in Australia, there was "mass scenes of hysteria", according to the police, after J-Bieb was forced to cancel an appearance in Sydney!

The police also reported that ten girls fainted as they waited overnight to catch Justin — and paramedics had to treat several injured fans, including one who fractured their kneecap! Ouch!

BIEBER FANS RIOT!

■ Justin was due to play a gig in a mall in NY — until thousands of fans turned up and started causing chaos, forcing him to cancel the gig!

Hundreds of JB's fans caused a stampede and a girl even had to be hospitalised after being trampled by the crowd!

Then, several fights broke out and the police had to be called in to control the crowd!

Following the mayhem, Justin's manager was arrested after he refused to Tweet that the gig was cancelled! Wow!

THE CRAZIEST BIEBER FANS EVER!

There have been loads of reports of zany J-Bieb fans! Check these out!

■ A 34-year-old forklift driver tried to prove that he is Justin's No. 1 fan by paying £250 a year for a 'BIEBER' personalised license plate — weird!

■ Justin fans camped for over 48 hours in NY for a free gig. One fan had travelled over 17 hours to get there!

■ Bieber fans took to Twitter to insult an Australian TV presenter after he reported that Justin was rude and even swore at one of the show's staff!

■ After Twitter changed their trending rules to stop Justin being at number one for, like, forever, his fans started calling him other names like Twieber so that he could keep trending on the site! Are they dedicated or what?!

BIEBER FEVER GETS SCARY!

■ Justin Bieber had to plead to his wacky fans to stop sending death threats to Kim Kardashian, after the rumour mill went wild that Justin and Kim were dating!

After Kim posted on Twitter that she had Bieber fever, and Justin posted up a pic of them saying that she was his girlfriend, stacks of JB fans started sending horrible tweets to Kim! Eventually, it got so bad that Justin had to send a message out asking them to stop, because he and Kim were just friends!

JUSTIN'S AIRPORT DRAMA!

■ When Justin arrived at a New Zealand airport, he was mobbed by hundreds of screaming fans, desperate to see their idol! Then, as he was rushed away by security, some of his fevered fans knocked over his mum and one over-excited fan even stole one of his favourite caps!

Luckily, Justin's mum wasn't seriously hurt, but J-Bieb Tweeted the next day, *Finally got to New Zealand last night. The airport was crazy. Not happy that someone stole my hat and knocked down my mama. Come on people.*

TROUBLE PROOF YOUR LIFE!

Check out our quick-fix tips for getting out of a fix… quick!

LADS

THE TROUBLE So you're chatting away to your BFF, telling her how much you looove your crush, when you realise he's standing behind you and has heard every word! Even the really cringey bit where you said he'd make a great husband!

THE TROUBLE TIP Laugh immediately to show you're not embarrassed, and say, "Oops! Didn't see you there! Let's pretend that never happened!" He'll be impressed with your laid-back attitude — and at least now he knows exactly how you feel! So it's not *all* bad…

SCHOOL

THE TROUBLE Your teacher catches you yawning in class, and when he asks if he's boring you, you mutter "Yes" under your breath... which your teacher hears — eek!

THE TROUBLE TIP Pretend you actually said "As if!" and explain that you were up all night studying super-hard for his class, and that's why you just couldn't hold in that yawn! That sounds believable, right…?

MATES

THE TROUBLE You feel like your bezzie has been out with every boy on the scene, and when she tells you about her latest crush, you crack and bitchily say, "There won't be any boys left for me at the rate you're going through them!"

THE TROUBLE TIP Even if you meant it as a joke, your mate could take serious offence at this! If she looks upset, add that you're not surprised she's popular with boys, because she's so much fun. Try to keep your jealous streak to yourself next time!

PARENTS

THE TROUBLE After a heated argument with one of the 'rents, you reach boiling point and scream, "I hate you! You're ruining my life!", before running off to your room!

THE TROUBLE TIP Most teens will end up saying something like this at some point, but that doesn't mean it won't hurt parents' feelings.

Once both of you have calmed down, try speaking to them alone and apologise. Explain that you definitely didn't mean what you said, and that you're just feeling a bit stressed out. Hopefully after a chat, everything will be sorted out!

skin tone — sorted!

SHAKE UP THE COLOURS YOU WEAR WITH OUR ULTIMATE SKIN TONE GUIDE!

spice girl
FLORENCE WELCH

Hair: Red, blonde or brown.
Eyes: Hazel, brown or green.
Skin: Pale, burns easily and may have freckles.
Make-up Magic: You'll look lush in neutral or spicy shades... Think brown and gold!
Colour Catastrophe: Pink might clash with your hair...

beautyuk Metallic Sparks Eyeliner in Gold.

Prestige Sunflower Illuminating Bronzing Powder.

your make-up kit!

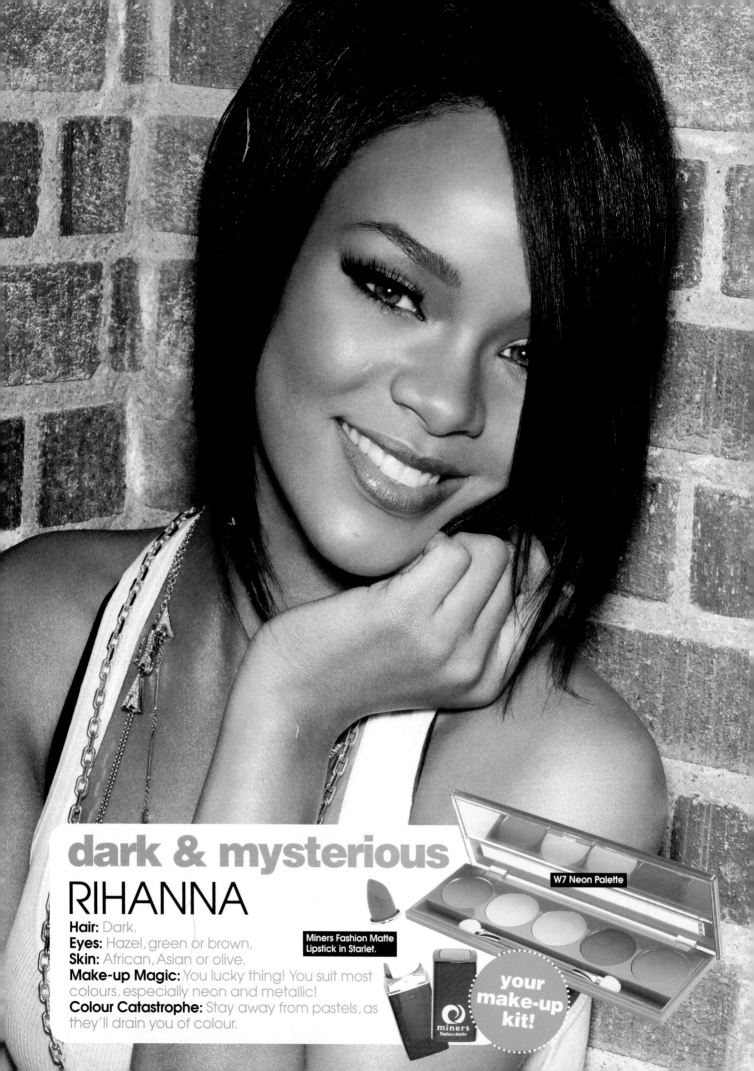

dark & mysterious

RIHANNA

Hair: Dark.
Eyes: Hazel, green or brown.
Skin: African, Asian or olive.
Make-up Magic: You lucky thing! You suit most colours, especially neon and metallic!
Colour Catastrophe: Stay away from pastels, as they'll drain you of colour.

W7 Neon Palette

Miners Fashion Matte Lipstick in Starlet.

your make-up kit!

O.P.I Nail Lacquer in What's With The Cattitude.

your make-up kit!

Barry M Deluxe Eyeshadow Kit.

blue belle

EMMA WATSON

Hair: Blonde or brown.
Eyes: Grey, green or hazel.
Skin: Fair to medium.
Make-up Magic: You look better than anyone else wearing blue. Experiment with turquoise, aqua, cornflower and electric blue!
Colour Catastrophe: Drastic colours like neon and loadsa kohl should be avoided...

BAG THAT BOY!

YOU'RE ONLY SIX STEPS AWAY FROM BAGGING YOUR CRUSH!

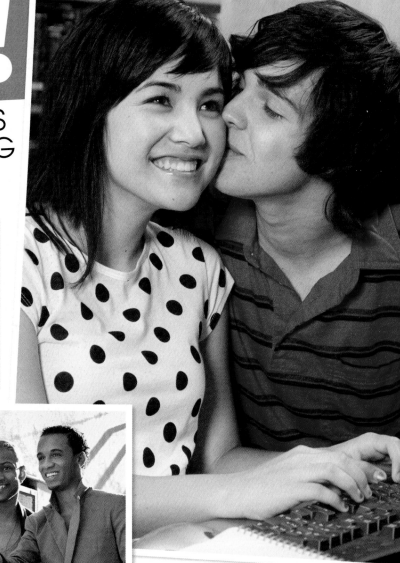

DON'T BE A STALKER...

Avoid looking like a stalker by making sure you do your own thing! If he's busy with band practice or plays footie at lunch time then DO NOT toddle along and pretend you left your jumper there after P.E.! He'll see right through you (trust us... he will) and he might also think you're a bit of a loser. The clingier than clingfilm look is not cool.

DON'T AGREE WITH HIM...

What's the point in dating someone if they're just going to nod and smile like one of those silly nodding dogs, huh?

If you've got the guts to disagree with him about stuff, he'll realise that you're confident and know your own mind.

So if he's slagging JLS, don't sit there like a filthy traitor and sigh, "I totally agree with you"... tell him straight!

DO HAVE A GIGGLE...

Boys aren't impressed with girls who moon around with a big ol' pout on their face! How many lads do you know who fancy moody Mrs Beckham?!

Turn that frown upside down and have a giggle with your mates... super-smart science boffins have informed us that signals will be sent to his brain telling him you're loadsa fun! Yay!

DON'T CROWD HIM...

Having a big posse of peeps around might make YOU feel more comfortable chatting to your crush — but put yourself in his shoes!

You may think that ten of your friends roaring hysterically at all his rubbish jokes is reeeally helpful... but he probably feels like he's stumbled into an audition for *The X Factor*! Not good.

DO MAKE EYE CONTACT...

You're not going to get very far if you can't even look at your crush! We're not saying that you have to, like, stare into his eyes like you're trying to hypnotise him into hearting you or something... but a bit of eyeball to eyeball action is always good.

Looking away occassionally or twiddling with your hair will also earn you bonus points!

DO LISTEN TO HIM...

If you do manage to corner him for a chat then use your moment wisely! You might think it's the perfect time to drop some HUGE hints about how awesome you are... but how about asking him what *he's* been up to?

If he thinks you're interested in his likes and dislikes then he'll just want to keep on talking... and talking... and talking! Result!

What's Your Top Mate STYLE?

WHAT IS IT ABOUT YOU THAT ALWAYS MAKES YOUR MATES SMILE?

START

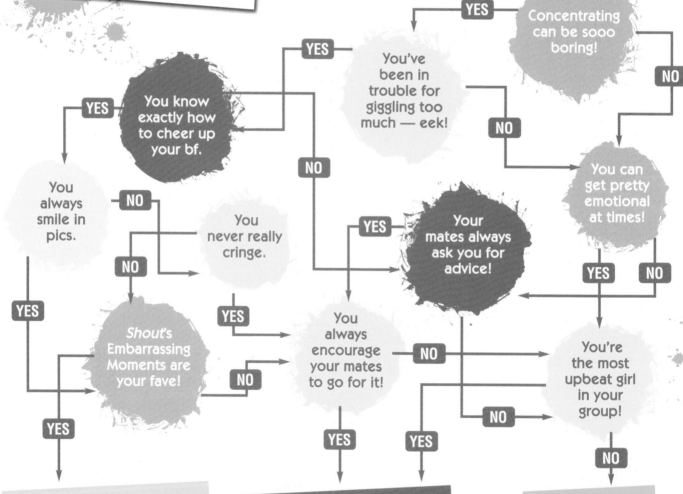

YES → Concentrating can be sooo boring!
NO →

You've been in trouble for giggling too much — eek!

You know exactly how to cheer up your bf.

YES

You always smile in pics.

NO You never really cringe.

NO

YES Your mates always ask you for advice!

You can get pretty emotional at times!

YES **NO**

YES *Shout's* Embarrassing Moments are your fave!

YES

NO

You always encourage your mates to go for it!

NO

You're the most upbeat girl in your group!

YES **YES** **NO**

NO

Sense of humour!

You've got a cheeky smile and you're always up to no good — but, hey, you can't be serious, like, all the time! Whenever your pals need to let off steam and have a total scream, they go to where the fun's at... That's where you step in!

Positive attitude!

It doesn't matter what you come up against... whether it's a tricky exam, a new make-up look or asking a lad out — you're always super-confident, no matter what! Plus, you share your happy vibes with your pals, leaving them feeling chirpier, too!

Big heart!

You're forever playing agony aunt to your mates and you're always the first person they turn to for help. But do ya know why? Cos you're sensitive and always understanding of their problems! Every girl needs a friend like you... including us!

LITTLE BOOTS

STEP OUT IN THE LATEST STYLES!

Linzi Shoes.

Linzi Shoes.

Linzi Shoes.

WE ♥ THIS COLOUR!

PIXIE LOTT'S BIKER BOOTS TOUGHEN UP HER GIRLIE DRESS.

Matalan.

Miss Selfridge.

FAUX SHEEPSKIN IS TOTALLY ON-TREND!

Matalan.

F&F at Tesco.

New Look.

Schuh.

VINTAGE VIBES!

Jane Norman.

dating:
real life V hollywood!

If only finding a bf was as easy as it is in the movies, sigh...

MYTH 1... The Fail-safe Flirting!

Hollywood — All she has to do is throw one measly little glance in his direction and he'll spend the rest of the movie daydreaming about her! She'll probably walk into a lamp post or whatever... but, naturally, he'll find it 'endearing' and fancy her even more! Tsk!

Real Life — The boys we know are a lil' bit more slow about the love stuff... so unless you want to spell it out for him (I-L-I-K-E-Y-O-U sounds a bit silly, right?), don't expect any attention anytime soon! And offering us leftover chips doesn't count as flirting either.

MYTH 2... The Perfect First Kiss!

Hollywood — No-one ever has an awkward first kiss in the movies! It doesn't matter if they're puckering up in a room full of people or if their bf is resisting the urge to bite them (yes Bella — we mean you!), their smooches always go super smoothly! How?

Real Life — You missed his mouth? Your mates are two metres away and shamelessly sniggering? You can still taste that tuna sandwich he had for lunch? Hmmm... just remember that movies don't show, like, the zillion takes they took to get it right!

MYTH 3... *The Ridiculous Romance!*

Hollywood — Such 'romantic gestures' typically involve trekking across the world for one lil' kiss... or serenading the lucky laydee in the school corridor! *Bella* even managed to bag a marriage proposal! We don't think you should hold your breath for that...

Real Life — Oh dear... where do we even start? He might decide to wear clean underwear if you're lucky! If any boys did serenade us we bet it would be that weirdo boy we're always trying to avoid — rather than our fave member of *The Wanted*! Boo!

MYTH 4... *The Fairytale Ending!*

Hollywood — It doesn't matter how many make-ups and break-ups they have, the couple always conclude that they belong together and it all works out in the end! Cue a happy ending with assorted sunshine, flowers and bunny rabbits. And a big fat snog at the end, too!

Real Life — Some of our 'relationships' are over before the movie credits roll — and most peeps will barely make the two-month mark! There's no shame in it, though... who wants to be bogged down with boys 24/7? Especially boys that don't change their pants? Not us!

"MY OCD NIGHTMARE!"

Chelsea Thwaite went to extreme measures to try to cope with stress…

Ever since I was little, I've always been, well, a little bit particular about things. Like when I had a meal, my glass would always have to be at a certain point on the mat, and when I ate my food, I had to do it in a certain order — from the thing I liked least, going clockwise round the plate.

"However, my obsession with doing things a certain way came to a head last year — just before I went back to school after summer.

"I'd sat some tests before the holidays that would determine which class I'd be going in to the following school year. I spent the whole summer worrying about whether I'd be in the same classes as my mates or not.

"I began to make bets with myself which, if I won them, meant that I would be in the same class as my friends. For example, when I had a shower, I'd check the time before I got in, and if I wasn't out before the minute hand got to the next number on the clock, I wouldn't be in the same class as my friends.

"I also became obsessed with doing things six times. If I had to lock the door, I'd lock and unlock it six times, and then check it another six times. Or if I was washing my hands, I'd have to do it six times — in really hot water and with antibacterial soap, so that I couldn't catch any germs. Although I knew I was being excessive, I felt as though I had to do it for things to stay normal in my life.

"However, doing every single daily task six times was really tiring, and washing my hands so often had made my skin dry and cracked. It was so painful to use antibacterial soap on my hands — but that didn't stop me.

"It wasn't until one day, when I'd been feeling particularly stressed out, my mum asked me to help prepare dinner. I started chopping up some vegetables, cutting each piece six times. My mum said she wanted them cut in to chunkier pieces, so she took the knife out of my hand and started chopping the vegetables roughly. The panic at the thought of having to eat the vegetables that hadn't been cut in the way I liked was too much, and I lost the plot!

"After Mum had managed to calm me down, she told me that she'd noticed I'd been acting strangely, and asked me to tell her what was wrong. I explained that I knew I'd been doing certain things obsessively, but that I felt I couldn't stop without something bad happening…

"We arranged for an appointment at the doctors', who said that he thought I was showing signs of obsessive compulsive disorder (OCD) — where people feel that they have to do certain things over and over again, often to make sure nothing bad happens to them or their family.

"I broke down in tears as the doctor asked me questions — I was scared, but also relieved that there was a reason for the way I'd been feeling and acting recently.

"I was referred for a special form of treatment that tries to train you to act differently during times of stress — so rather than do something repeatedly when I feel stressed, I now try to find other ways to relax my mind.

"It's taken a long time, but it seems to be working — I still have urges to check a door six times to make sure it's been locked properly, but now, so that I don't, I talk myself through locking and shutting the door, so my mind can be in no doubt that I've done it right.

"Although I'm still on the road to recovery, I know that with more therapy, and support from my family, I'll hopefully manage to come through it all…"

> "I became obsessed with doing things six times"

> "I broke down in tears in the doctors office"

HELP BOX

If you're feeling stressed out — whether about school, mates, boys or home life — the best thing to do is to talk about your feelings with someone you trust. By explaining how you're feeling to someone else, you'll be able to see what exactly is making you feel stressed — and then you should be able to work out a solution to help try to get things back on track.

If you think you might have OCD, or are feeling worried about how you're coping with stress and anxiety, see your GP — they'll have dealt with this plenty of times before, and will be able to help.

WHAT'S YOUR MOAN ZONE?

Are you sitting on that moan throne again?!

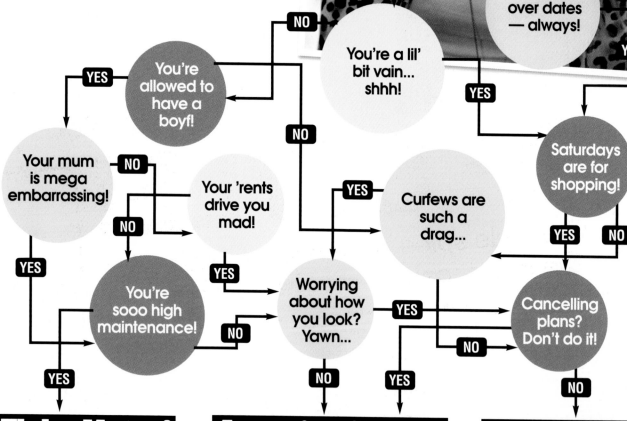

START

Mates over dates — always!

NO → You're a lil' bit vain... shhh!

YES → Saturdays are for shopping!

YES → You're allowed to have a boyf!

NO (from You're a lil' bit vain) → You're allowed to have a boyf!

YES (from You're allowed to have a boyf) → Your mum is mega embarrassing!

NO → Your 'rents drive you mad!

Your mum is mega embarrassing!
NO → You're sooo high maintenance!
YES → (down)

Your 'rents drive you mad!
YES → Worrying about how you look? Yawn...

Curfews are such a drag...
YES → (to Curfews)

Saturdays are for shopping!
YES / NO → Cancelling plans? Don't do it!

You're sooo high maintenance!
NO → Worrying about how you look? Yawn...
YES → (down)

Worrying about how you look? Yawn...
YES → Cancelling plans? Don't do it!
NO → (down)

Curfews are such a drag...
YES → (down)

Cancelling plans? Don't do it!
NO → (down)

Flaky Mates!

As far as you're concerned, the weekends are for chilling out with your friends! So when they call you up bleating about dates, you're not happy! Try not to be too hard on 'em, though... what happens when you get asked out, huh?

Annoying 'Rents!

Sigh... everything would be so much easier if your parents just let you do what you want! You're not allowed to wear make-up, they're crazy strict about curfews... AND you're not allowed to have a boyfriend! You. Want. To. Scream. Aaargh!

Bad Hair Day!

You're only happy when your hair's lookin' hot — and if your barnet doesn't want to play ball then you'll be in a bad mood for the rest of the day! Try not to be such a fusspot, though... you can still have fun with messy hair! Bed head rules!

All products available at time of press.

THE a-z OF STYLE!

Our style spies have been scouting for the latest fashion and beauty buys…

33

a

ANIMAL PRINT

Inject some punk into your look with bold leopard, snake and zebra print!

Make-up bag, Next.

Boohoo.

Generation 915 at New Look.

Corioliss Couture Python Edition Straighteners.

Pixie Lott

npw Nail Polish Remover Pads.

Fruity fragrance
30 pcs
Nail Polish Remover pads
Gentle & Effective - alcohol and acetone free

Rebel Nails in Pink Cheetah.

Peel on, Peel off Nail Sensation

Glamorous Nails in 5 minutes

NO MORE... Drying, Smudging or Chipping

Colourworks Fabulous Files.

b

BIG & BOLD

Add a splash (or two!) of bold colour to really liven things up! We love pink, blue, green and orange on nails and eyes — just remember to tone down the rest of your make-up!

Collection 2000 Colour Intense Trio in Lemon Tropics.

Jane Norman.

Tommy Hillfiger Loud For Her.

Sleek MakeUP Limited Edition Eyeshadow Palette in Circus.

Bourjois Volumizer Mascara.

Glee Divas Free Your Glee Nail Set.

Nike at La Redoute.

35

C

CANDY COLOURS

Pastels are gonna be hot news this year, so go for baby pinks and blues and sorbet shades of peach and lemon, and get ready to look mouth-wateringly gorgeous!

Barry M Trio Eyeshadow in Pretty Pastels.

Bourjois Blush in Rose Coup de Foudre.

Models Own Pretty Baby Duo Eyeshadow.

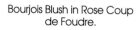

Bags of Sparkle.

Rare.

Alwear.

O.P.I Nail Lacquer in Rumples Wiggin.

Sleek MakeUP Dip-it Eyeliner in Pink.

⭐

d

DRESS UP

Ah, don't you just love getting ready for a night out?! All the primping and preening and dancing about… It's sometimes better than the party itself! Here's how we take care of things…

■ Remember a hint of tan on your arms and legs.
■ A gorgeous dress with chipped nails? Don't even think about it, missy!
■ Primer makes foundation easier to put on and gives your skin a little glow.

Primark Prime Of Your Life Face Primer.

Primark Bloominous Illuminator.

Rimmel Sun Shimmer Instant Tan.

Boots French Manicure Kit.

Miners Beauty Brilliance Highlighter Stick in Pixie.

New Look.

George at ASDA.

Internacionale.

Internacionale.

Schwarzkopf Professional Osis Shine Duster.

Cherry Carmex Moisturising Lip Balm.

SPF 15

CHERRY
CARMEX
TRADE NAME REG.

MOISTURISING LIP BALM

IT SOOTHES.
IT RELIEVES.
IT MOISTURISES.

www.mycarmex.com

e✪
EVERYDAY ESSENTIALS

When we're keeping our look casual, we sling on our fave skinny jeans, tie our hair back in a messy bun, then add a hint of our fave no make-up make-up!

2true Smooth Matte Pressed Powder

2true Smooth Matte Pressed Powder.

Maybelline Pure Cover Mineral Concealer.

Technic Natural Lashes Clear Mascara.

e.l.f. Eyeshadow Duo

e.l.f. Eyeshadow Duo.

Palmolive Soft & Gentle Eden Passion Flower.

Tigi Rockaholic Dirty Secret Dry Shampoo.

Alexa Chung

Jane Norman.

Johnson's 3-in-1 Facial Cleansing Wipes.

Boohoo.

Colorsport 24 Hour Eyeliner.

V05 Ultimate Hold Weather Resistant Hairspray.

f

FESTIVAL FABULOUS

Heading to a festival? Then get the A-list look with cute sundresses and sandals. Dry shampoo and cleansing wipes are also a must, and make sure you have a pair of wellies in case it rains!

g

GOTHIC GLAM

Black, plum, silver, gold and red — those are the colours you should be wearing if you're gonna rock the goth trend. If you're not brave enough to do dark lipstick, wear it on your nails instead — problem solved!

Fascinator, Accessorize.

Nicole by O.P.I Nail Lacquer in Show You Care.

True Colour Lipstick in Mulberry.

Max Factor Smoky Eye Effect Eyeshadow in Silver Storm.

Evie at Peacocks.

Freedom at Topshop.

Accessorize.

Scarlett & Crimson Boom Lash Volumising Mascara.

Peaches for PPQ at Very.

Lush Happy Hippy Hair & Body Gel.

Oy! Shampoo & Shower.

ASOS.

Emma Roberts

Love Hair Extensions Braid Band.

REF Ocean Mist.

h

HIPPY CHIC

This trend gets us right in the mood for summer, but you can still do it in winter, girls. Pleat the front section of your hair or fringe, and pin back, then gently curl the rest to create messy waves.

Water Aid for H&M.

Bumble & Bumble Alojoba Conditioner.

Accessorize.

SWISS

COLLECTION BY

IRRE-SWISS-ABLES

MINI NAIL LACQUERS | MINIS FLACONS DE NAIL LACQUERS
MINI ESMALTES | MINI NAGELLACKE

O·P·I

O.P.I Swiss Collection
Mini Nail Lacquers.

ICE QUEEN

Go all snow queen on us
with Alpine knits, furry mitts,
and icy-cold colours. You'll
be cooler than ice!

GOSH Extreme
Art Eye Liner.

17 Va Va Voom
Plumping Lip
Gloss in Nude.

THE BODY SHOP

ICE BLUE
BLEU GIVRE

SHAMPOO

SHAMPOOING

ALL HAIR TYPES / TOUS TYPES DE CHEVEUX

250 ml (8.4 US FL OZ)

The Body Shop Ice
Blue Shampoo.

17 Fast Finish
Nail Polish in
Smoky
Marble.

Alwear.

New Look.

Dorothy Perkins.

New Look.

j

JEAN-IOUS

OK, so you can't turn denim into a beauty trend…. But you can wear some awesome blue make-up! We love peacock blue eyeshadow for a punchy make-up update!

Rimmel Glam Eyes Mono Eyeshadow in Posh Peacock.

Miners Liquid Liner in Blue.

Sleek MakeUP Eye Dust.

Alwear.

Liquid Line

Office.

Miss Selfridge.

LCN Nail Care in Paparazzi.

Nail Care

LCN

NAIL POLISH

43

Vendula.

Paul & Joe Lipstick.

Double Dip Orange & Cherry Flavour Lip Care.

k

KITSCH

The *Shout* girlies love anything retro or vintage — here are our fave Katy Perry-style picks!

Eyeko Beauty Tea Rose Polish.

Crafted at Republic.

Accessorize Jumbo Eye Crayon No. 5.

Peacocks.

Corioliss Floral Vintage Hairdryer.

Alwear.

Primark Kiss Me Lips Lipbalm.

BEAUTIFUL
COLOUR COSMETICS

KISS ME LIPS
LIPBALM

Accessorize.

Matalan.

LOVE

Lush Strawberry Feels
Forever Soap.

Eyeko
Petite
Polish
For French Nails

Eyeko Beauty
Petite Polish.

Internacionale.

Trésor
IN LOVE

LANCÔME
PARIS

Tresor In Love by
Lancome.

Miners Crystal Crush
Lipgloss in Heartbreaker.

crystal crush
LIGHT REFLECTING LIPGLOSS

miners

LOVE
All you need is love...
and to heart these
gorgeous buys!

45

m

MMMM, METALLIC

Look like a million dollars without the million dollar price tag! Grab a glitzy dress or try our fave party trick — after creating a smoky eye, blend shimmer dust into the inside corner of your eye!

Taylor Swift

Lee Stafford Colour Xtreme Glitzy Gold Glitter Spray.

Famous by Sue Moxley Eye Palette in Mystical.

Boohoo.

17 Solo Eyeshadow in Gold Emerald.

Jane Norman.

Collection 2000 Colour Intense Trio in Silver Storm.

George at ASDA.

n

NEON NIGHTS
Wake up your make-up with a punchy hit of neon. Just take it easy when you're applying the rest of your slap...

Miss Selfridge.

Rocket Dog.

2true Duo Eyeshadow No. 8.

W7 Neon Palette.

LTD.

W7 Neon Lights Eyeliner.

missguided.co.uk.

47

Accessorize.

Miners Fashion Matte Lipstick in Coral.

River Island.

17 Fast Finish Nail Polish in Nail Garnet.

Selena Gomez

OLD-SCHOOL GLAMOUR
This look channels old-school movie stars like Marilyn Monroe...Think LBD, perfectly manicured nails and pillar box red lips. Vamp it up, girl!

Rimmel Exaggerate Eye Liner.

Schwarzkopf Professional Osis Glamour Queen Hairspray.

Babyliss Glamour Waves Curling Tongs.

Red Label.

Accessorize.

48

Boohoo.

Matalan.

Sleek MakeUP Blush In Pink Pixie.

Internacionale.

Alwear.

River Island.

Maybelline Forever Strong Professional Nail Varnish in Flamand Rose.

W7 Candy Floss Blush.

CANDY FLOSS

PINK
Pink makes the boys wink, so add some to your look! Try a cute corsage or wear pink blush with pastel lipgloss. Yum!

49

Poundland Chit Chat Power Lash Mascara.

Alberto Balsam Anti-oxidant Blueberry Conditioner.

Primark.

George at ASDA.

Montagne Jeunesse Strawberry Souffle Masque.

Skin Therapy 3 In 1 Fragranced Facial Wipes.

So…? Desirable Body Fragrance.

q

QUIDS IN

You can get a lot of cute buys that'll spruce up your wardrobe from only £1 (Primark, anyone?)! Go shopping once a month for these little treats!

Frankie Sandford

Matalan.

r

ROCK CHICK
Let your inner Hayley Williams out with loads of eyeliner, textured hair and a studded biker jacket. You rock!

Rebel Hair Collection Limited Edition Hearts & Swallows Straighteners.

George at ASDA.

Barry M Lip Lacquer Crayon No. 3.

George at ASDA.

Crafted at Republic.

Avril Lavigne Forbidden Rose.

SCARLETT & CRIMSON
Be you tattoo
12 unique tattoo transfers
Be Your Own Scene!
12 unique designs

Scarlett & Crimson Be You Tattoo.

Crafted at Republic.

51

Ke$ha

F&F at Tesco.

S

SHIMMER, SPARKLE & SHINE

Any diva will tell you that it's all about the sparkles! Grab a glitter dust, sweep over your eyelids, then add fake lashes. Make-up = done!

Star Gazer Glitter Stars

BarryM Glitter Lashes in Green.

Red Label.

Office.

George at ASDA Light Up My Life! Luminous Highlighter.

Emani Minerals Glitter Dust.

Accessorize.

Own The Runway.

BIG EYEBROWS

COLORSPORT

SPECIALLY SHAPED NIB

EYEBROW DEFINER
8 HOUR COLOUR

BROWN

NATURAL COLOUR
SMOOTH EVEN LINE
LONG WEARING FORMULA
EASY PRECISE APPLICATION
Minimum effort maximum impact

Colorsport Eyebrow Definer in Brown.

GOTH LIPS

Plump Your Pucker Tinted Gloss in Razz My Berry.

Matalan.

HOT DESIGNER FRAGRANCES

DKNY Love From New York.

love from New York

DKNY

MINERAL MAKE-UP

ROCK FACE MINERALS

Rock Face Face Minerals Foundation.

Alwear.

Soul Cal at Republic.

NUDE NAILS

REVLON

31706

D.I.Y NAILS

Ms:Pedicure Best In Toe.

Revlon Nail Enamel in Gray Suede.

Very.co.uk.

Ms Pedicure Best In Toe.

6 picks for a perfect pedi

Primark.

t ★

2012'S TOP 10 TRENDS
Here's what we're gonna be lovin' next year...!

u

UNDERNEATH YOUR CLOTHES

Keep your skin looking tip-top and treat yourself to some gorgeous undies!

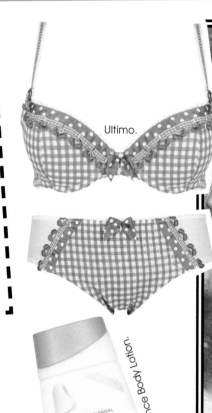

Ultimo.

Beautifully Delicious Honey & Almond Scrublicious Body Scrub.

n-spa Apple Mint Crunch Shower & Bath Gel.

E45 Endless Moisture Radiance Body Lotion.

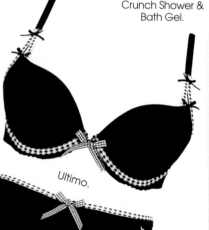

Ultimo.

Palmer's Cocoa Butter Formula Natural Bronze Body Lotion.

Ultimo.

The Body Shop Coconut Body Butter.

54

F&F at Tesco.

Mememe Single Eyeshadow.

George at ASDA.

Apricot.

Matalan.

17 Eyes

17 Solo Eyeshadow in Violet Rock.

MAXFACTOR
MAX EFFECT
MINI NAIL POLISH

Max Factor Max Effect Mini Nail Polish in Diva Violet.

V

VIOLET
This colour is super-glam — we love wearing it to break up an all-black outfit!

GOSH

GOSH Velvet Touch Waterproof Eyeliner.

French Connection.

55

Soul Cal at Republic.

2true Duo Eyeshadow.

Primark.

Autograph at M&S.

New Look.

George at ASDA Velvet Eyeshadow.

W

WHITE
Make sure you keep your look pure and simple with this season's statement shade.

White eyeshadow's like sprinkling icing sugar on to a cake — it keeps your look pretty but understated.

2true Eyeshadow Dazzler.

GOSH Glamorous Eyeshadow.

Evie at Peacocks.

GOSH Kohl Eyeliner.

French Connection.

X

XTRA SPECIAL
These are on our wish list. Now we've just got to wait for Santa to hurry up and get here!

PAUL'S BOUTIQUE
24/7
Eau de Toilette
3 x 10 ml. 0.34 FL OZ ℮

Paul's Boutique 24/7 Eau de Toilette.

French Connection.

St Tropez Tan Optimiser Body Butter.

Lipsy.

Juicy Couture Eau de Parfum.

wild blackberry blossom

Philosophy Wild Blackberry Blossom Body Lotion.

Urban Outfitters.

CLINIQUE long last glosswear SPF 15 gloss longtemps SPF 15

Clinique Long Last Glosswear.

Office.

Kristen Stewart

Debenhams.

Abandon at USC.

Y

YELLOW
Yellow's an amazing colour for mixing up a look. We guarantee that every time you see this sunny shade, you'll smile!

Models Own Duo Eyeshadow in Neon Zest.

n-spa Lemon Cleansing Fruit Fix Hand Wash.

lemon cleansing fruit fix hand wash

"Give a girl a lemon" said the wise and she will add some sugar make you the sweetest of lemonad should you dabble in the zest o most playful of fruits then be prep to emerge from the water unavoid and deliciously edible."

500ml ℮ 16.9floz   n-s   FRU

Matalan.

Matalan.

Lush Bath Bomb in Fizzbanger.

N.Y.C Long-wearing Nail Enamel in Yellow.

N...C
NEW YORK COLORS
Long-Wearing Nail Enamel
i114A
13 ml ℮

Models Own Eyeliner in Neon Yellow.

Blowfish.

Simple Radiance Brightening Eye Make-up Remover Pads.

Marks & Spencer.

Umberto Giannini Overnight Beauty Moisture Balm.

La Senza.

Store Twenty One.

Young & Pure Face Cream.

Superdrug Deep Action Cleansing Lotion.

Simple Soothing Facial Toner.

Jane Norman.

Z

Zzzz

These are our essential bed-time beauty rules....

■ ALWAYS take your make-up off before bed. If you're too tired to use a cleansing lotion, just use make-up remover pads.

■ Toner helps to get rid of dirt that's stuck deep in your pores so we try to use ours every night.

■ Never forget to moisturise. You'll wake up with silky smooth skin in the morning. What could be better?!

59

WHAT WOULD YOU DO? TICK THE BOX THAT'S RIGHT FOR YOU!

THE FRIEND FACTOR!

GREAT MATE OR MATE HATE? FIND OUT BELOW...

1. YOUR MATE WANTS YOU TO WATCH HER BOYF PLAY FOR THE SCHOOL FOOTIE TEAM BUT YOU THINK SPORTS ARE BORING. YOU...

☐ Tell her 'no'! Well, her boyf's team will probably lose anyway!

☐ Go and stand in the pouring rain, in silence, listening to her bang on about how great he is!

☐ Go — and have fun checking out all the other buff boys!

2. YOU HEAR THAT YOUR BEZZIE HAS BEEN STARTING SOME RUMOURS ABOUT YOU BEHIND YOUR BACK. YOU...

☐ Start a life-wrecking rumour about her and laugh as she suffers!

☐ Tell everyone it's true, because you don't want to call her a liar...

☐ Talk to her about it and try to sort it out calmly!

3. IT'S THE HOTTEST PARTY OF THE YEAR AND YOUR MATE WANTS TO BORROW THE COOLEST OUTFIT IN YOUR WARDROBE! YOU SAY...

☐ Yeah, right... As if!

☐ Well, I was going to wear it, but it'll probably look better on you.

☐ Cool, but could I borrow your necklace to complete my killer outfit?

4. YOU ASK OUT HER CRUSH FOR HER, BUT HE SAYS HE WOULD RATHER EAT HIS OWN UNDERPANTS THAN GO ON A DATE WITH HER! YOU TELL HER...

☐ Everything he said — but with some painful add-ons, just for a laugh!

☐ That he's thinking about it, and that it's looking good!

☐ That she's way too good for him!

5. YOUR MATE HAS JUST TURNED UP WITH THE WORST HAIRCUT EVER! YOU...

☐ Burst out laughing, then ask if she cut it herself... with a lawnmower!

☐ Tell her that you love it sooo much!

☐ Hint that maybe the new 'do doesn't suit her as much as the last one.

6. YOU'VE JUST FOUND OUT THAT YOU AND YOUR BFF HAVE THE SAME CRUSH. YOU...

☐ Get in there before she does!

☐ Decide to fancy someone else, even though you don't really want to...

☐ Have a laugh with her, chatting about how hot that guy is!

7. YOUR CRUSH ASKS YOU TO THE CINEMA ON FRIDAY — BUT YOU'VE ALREADY ARRANGED TO CATCH A CHICK FLICK WITH YOUR BEZZIE! YOU...

☐ Ditch her! Your crush is way too hot to turn down!

☐ Tell him no, because you want to keep her happy...

☐ Arrange a big group trip to the cinema and keep everyone happy!

8. YOUR FRIEND HAS ASKED TO COPY YOUR HOMEWORK AGAIN, BUT YOU KNOW SHE WOULDN'T LET YOU DO THE SAME. YOU...

☐ Give her all of the wrong answers — that'll show her!

☐ Give in to her and be secretly annoyed!

☐ Suggest that you two should do your homework together in future.

MOSTLY PINK...

Wow! We're shocked that you actually have any mates! You always think of yourself first and for some freaky reason, you kinda enjoy dissing your bezzie and laughing at her problems... Time to play nice!

MOSTLY GREEN...

You're a bit of a wimp, really! You let your mates take advantage of your sweet nature and you need to stick up for yourself more. Try talking to your bezzie about how you feel more often.

MOSTLY BLUE...

It's official — you're a great mate! Keeping a good friendship is a high priority to you and you know that it's all about give and take. Plus, you're the best at helping out your mates when they need it the most. We wish we were your bezzie!

My Super SWEET 16!

THE PHRASE 'ALL ABOUT ME!' JUST TOOK ON A WHOLE NEW MEANING…

Last time we checked, our birthday celebrations weren't that big of a deal! We might get a few cards and a woolly jumper from our gran that we'll probably never wear… but we woudn't spend weeks thinking about it!

However, that doesn't seem to be the case for some teens when they turn 16… Apparently that turns you into a proper birthday brat — especially if the MTV show *My Super Sweet 16* is to be believed! Read all about it right here… gulp!

THE INVITATIONS...

Who knew that your invites would be such a big deal, huh? One teen decided to dish out mega-swish dog tag necklaces to every single person they'd invited! Kerching!

And another dude even sat on a judging panel with his mates and auditioned peeps from his school — Simon Cowell style! The cheek!

THE OUTFITS...

Ever heard the phrase, 'Money can't buy you style'? It was invented for these girlies, that's for sure!

One girl got a dress made that was *exactly* the same as one her fave celebs had worn... but someone forgot to mention that the original dress was freakin' horrible! We think we'll just stick to New Look, thanks.

Sorry... you just don't have the likeability factor!

THE ENTRANCE...

Our personal fave? The one when a girl thought it would be a great idea to paint her (brown) horse with white stripes... to make it look like a zebra! Huh?

Another great choice was when one dude chose to arrive in a plush limo with the delightful Danielle Lloyd. Ah, so *that's* what her job is! Good to know!

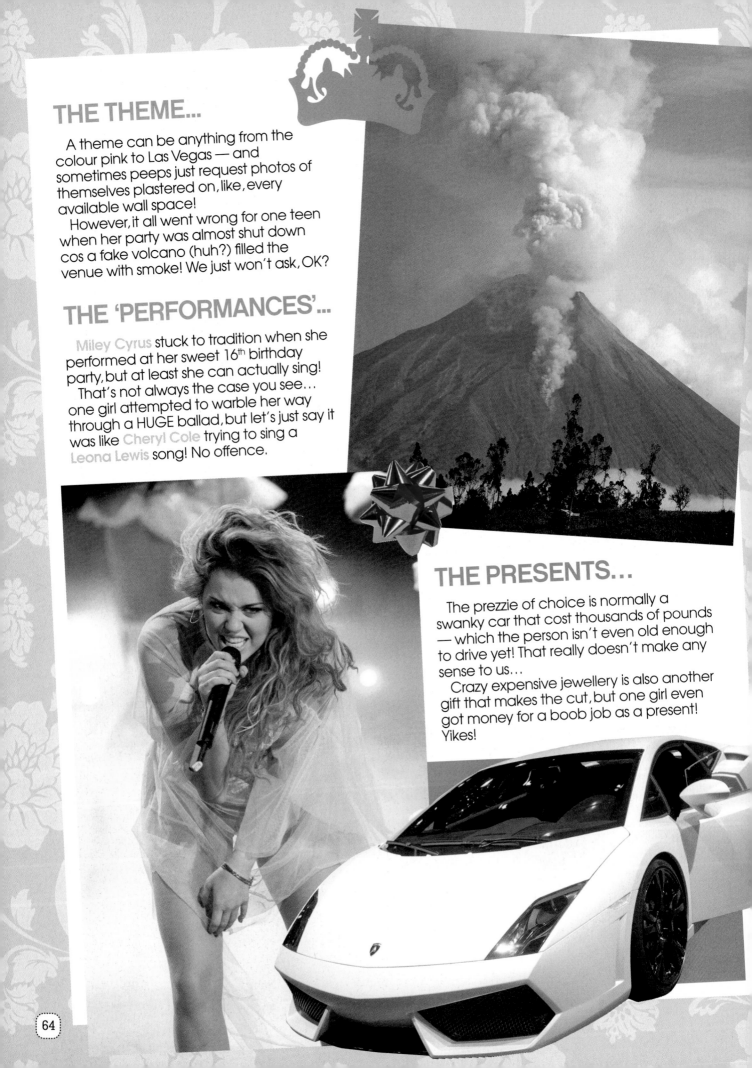

THE THEME...

A theme can be anything from the colour pink to Las Vegas — and sometimes peeps just request photos of themselves plastered on, like, every available wall space!

However, it all went wrong for one teen when her party was almost shut down cos a fake volcano (huh?) filled the venue with smoke! We just won't ask, OK?

THE 'PERFORMANCES'...

Miley Cyrus stuck to tradition when she performed at her sweet 16th birthday party, but at least she can actually sing!

That's not always the case you see… one girl attempted to warble her way through a HUGE ballad, but let's just say it was like Cheryl Cole trying to sing a Leona Lewis song! No offence.

THE PRESENTS...

The prezzie of choice is normally a swanky car that cost thousands of pounds — which the person isn't even old enough to drive yet! That really doesn't make any sense to us…

Crazy expensive jewellery is also another gift that makes the cut, but one girl even got money for a boob job as a present! Yikes!

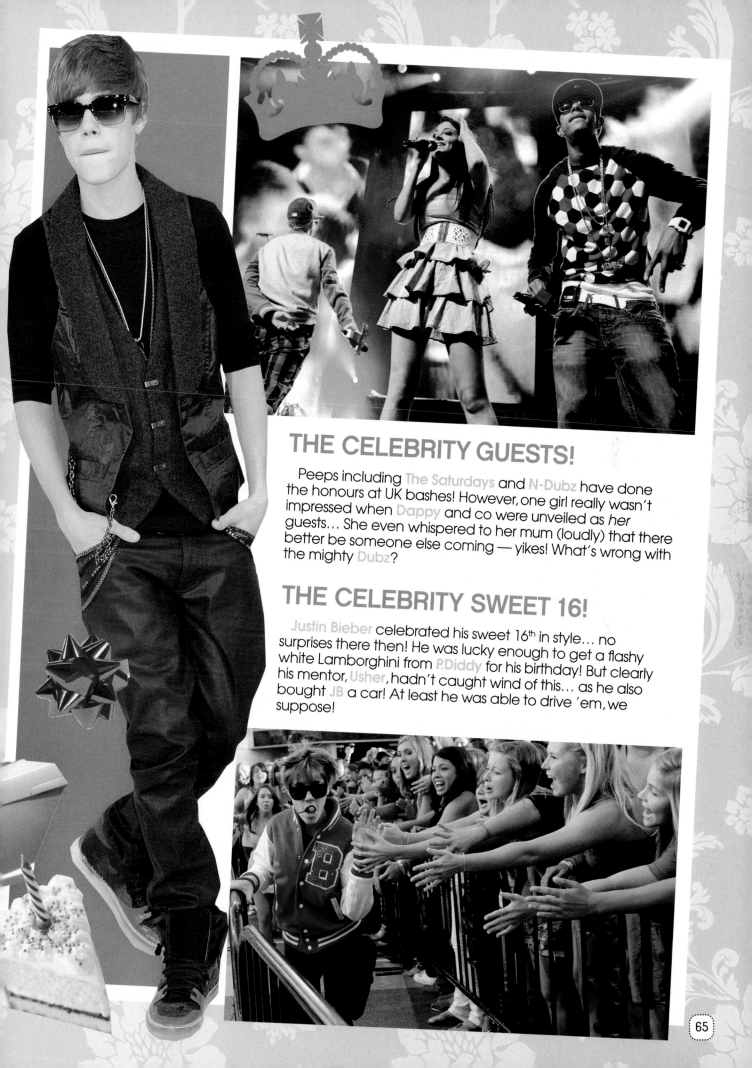

THE CELEBRITY GUESTS!

Peeps including The Saturdays and N-Dubz have done the honours at UK bashes! However, one girl really wasn't impressed when Dappy and co were unveiled as *her* guests… She even whispered to her mum (loudly) that there better be someone else coming — yikes! What's wrong with the mighty Dubz?

THE CELEBRITY SWEET 16!

Justin Bieber celebrated his sweet 16th in style… no surprises there then! He was lucky enough to get a flashy white Lamborghini from P.Diddy for his birthday! But clearly his mentor, Usher, hadn't caught wind of this… as he also bought JB a car! At least he was able to drive 'em, we suppose!

embarrassing
MOMENTS!

The only place that's safe for you to share your cringiest confessions!

cringe of the fortnight

"I looked up to see my brother and all his mates!"

£20 WINNER

"I'd just got out of the shower, and decided to listen to my iPod while I was wandering round getting ready.

"I couldn't find my shoes, but remembered I'd left them downstairs, so went to get them. I was only in a towel, but it didn't matter, cos it was only my mum and me in the house.

"I was singing along to my music as I walked into the living room, and I started dancing, too! Suddenly, someone ripped my headphones out of my ears, and I looked up to see my brother with all his mates! He'd been shouting at me to get out, but I hadn't heard! I don't know what's worse — the dancing, the singing, or the towel! Eek!"

Casey, Swansea 👀👀👀

CRINGE RATING

Illustration by Kirk Houston

MAJORLY MORTIFYING! 👀👀👀 KINDA CRINGEY! 👀👀 BARELY BLUSH-WORTHY! 👀

A Spot of Bother!

"I was going on holiday with my family, and we were going through security checks at the airport. I was quite nervous as we got ready to go through the scanner.

"There was a sign saying that belts should be removed, so I quickly took mine off. As it came to my turn to step through, I accidently stood on the bottom of my trousers, and they slipped down, exposing my bum! Everyone queuing up must have seen my spotty pants, and the security woman had a smirk across her face! Luckily my trousers didn't fall right down, but it was still super-cringey!"

Hollie, Oxford

Bowled Over!

"I was bowling with a group of mates, including my crush, and I was having loads of fun! Things were going well, and my team even won the game!

"When we finished playing, we went to grab some food to eat outside. I got a big plate of nachos and headed over to the door. Just as I was about to walk through it, my crush said something funny. I turned round to laugh, but as I turned back, I walked smack into a glass door! My nachos got squashed between me and the door, so were all down my top, and I got a huge bump on my head! My crush found it hilarious, but we're now going out — so maybe it was worth it!"

Josie, Portsmouth

On The Wrong Foot!

"One Monday morning, I woke up really late for school and rushed to get ready as quickly as I could. Luckily my mum gave me a lift, so I arrived just in time to run into registration.

"As I walked to my seat, one of the boys shouted out, 'Forgotten how to put shoes on, have you?!' and everyone started laughing! I looked down, and realised I'd put my shoes on the wrong feet! I've no idea how I didn't notice — but it must have been because I was in such a rush! I had to then swap them over in front of everyone, which is when the boy also pointed out I had odd socks on — oops!"

Bryony, Leeds 😊

Runaway Bra!

"I'd just had a swimming lesson during P.E. and was getting changed back into my school uniform. For some reason, I couldn't find my bra anywhere, and had to give up and go without it. Luckily I had a thick jumper on, so I didn't think anyone would notice.

"As I walked to my next lesson, I heard my P.E. teacher shouting my name. I turned round to see her waving my bra in the air and asking if I knew who might have left it behind. I really wanted to say no, because everyone was staring at me, but I kinda wanted my bra back! I quickly grabbed it and quietly said it was mine, but everyone was already staring at me! Mega cringe!"

Dani, London

Play-n Embarrassing!

"I was in English at school, and we were reading a really boring play. Everyone had been given parts to read out, and I had a rubbish, small one.

"I wasn't paying much attention, but suddenly I snapped out of my daydream and realised it was my turn to speak! I got my words muddled up and instead of shouting my line (which was 'Bye, Mum!') I shouted, 'My bum!'. The whole class erupted with hysterical laughter and the teacher got me into trouble because she thought I'd done it on purpose!"

Megan, Dumfries

67

WHAT DOES YOUR

facebook

SAY ABOUT YOU?

Find out what your profile pic says about you!

MATES!
If you've chosen a pic of you and your mates, it shows that friendship is mega-important to you!

BLACK AND WHITE!
You're totally stylish and want the world to know! A classic black and white pic shows that you're cool, confident and would love to strut your stuff down the catwalk!

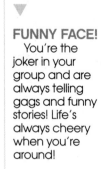

FUNNY FACE!
You're the joker in your group and are always telling gags and funny stories! Life's always cheery when you're around!

+ Upload Photos   + Upload Videos

CRINGEY PIC!

You never take yourself too seriously and are always game for a laugh! Which is lucky — cos you're a total EM magnet!

YOUR PET!

Is there anything cuter than your cat or dog sleeping in front of the telly? Nope, we didn't think so! Plus, we bet you have loads of funny pet vids on your page, too!

YOU AND YOUR BFF!

You guys are gonna be BFFL and you want the whole world to know! Show that you're super-BFFs by having matching pics on your profiles!

POSING!

You're mega-confident, and have no problems getting your flirt on! Well... when you look this good, why wouldn't you show off a little?!

YOU AND YOUR BOYF!

Awww! How slushy are you?! We bet your profile is covered in loads of cheesy messages about how cute he is, too!

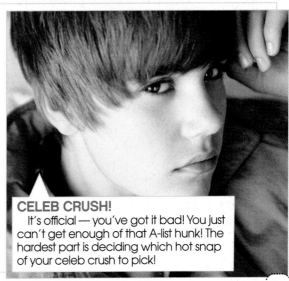

CELEB CRUSH!

It's official — you've got it bad! You just can't get enough of that A-list hunk! The hardest part is deciding which hot snap of your celeb crush to pick!

"MY SCHOOL SUSPENDED ME FOR KISSING!"

Chloe's PDA got her in serious hot water…

I've always been pretty confident with lads, so I wasn't too surprised when David, one of most popular guys in school, asked me out. I wanted to make sure everyone knew he was mine — so we were always holding hands and snogging in the middle of school! Everybody did it, so I wasn't going to be any different…

"HE BANNED COUPLES FROM KISSING IN SCHOOL."

"However, it wasn't long after this that our headmaster decided that it was getting out of hand… So he banned couples from kissing in the school grounds! Everyone thought it was ridiculous — it was none of the school's business what people did when they weren't in class. And what were people supposed to do, just stand next to each other and pretend that they weren't going out?!

"Everyone was talking about it and they all seemed to decide that they were just gonna ignore it. I felt the same… I wanted to kiss David whenever I wanted to, not when the teachers told me I could — and I didn't want David to think I was a goody-two shoes.

"I remember this really popular couple snogged in the middle of the classroom when the teacher nipped out of the room for a moment, and they got a massive round of applause! It was so funny — the teacher was just outside but she didn't have a clue what was going on…

"I DIDN'T WANT DAVID TO THINK I WAS A GOODY-TWO SHOES."

"I have to admit, the teachers did seem pretty strict about the whole thing. We'd already had another massive lecture on the no kissing

thing at the latest assembly, and one girl ended up in detention when she got caught! Her parents even made her dump her boyfriend because of it! I guess I just didn't think it would happen to me…

"David and I were hanging out one lunchtime, when the bell rang. Our classes were just across the hall from each other, so instead of having a cheeky snog outside like normal, we walked up together. We were holding hands and giggling, and when we got to the corridor, we turned to say goodbye…

"I guess I knew it was a bit stupid, but I really wanted to kiss him there and then — so I did! There were loads of people pushing past us and, I have to admit, it was kind of a thrill to know that everyone could see me snog my gorge boyf!

"IT WAS A THRILL TO SNOG MY GORGE BOYF IN FRONT OF EVERYONE."

"That was until I felt a tap on my shoulder and we were pulled apart — by my headmaster! I thought I was going to faint when I saw him glaring at us — he looked so angry and that's when I realised I was in massive trouble!

"He started shouting at us in the middle of the corridor — it was horrible! Everyone was looking at us as they walked past and I thought I was going to die of shame! The row seemed to go on forever, and then it got even worse…

"The headmaster made us come to his office, and said that he had no choice but to suspend us! David didn't seem to be bothered about the whole thing, but I was horrified — I knew my parents would be so disappointed with me…

"I KNEW MY PARENTS WOULD BE SO DISAPPOINTED."

"I was grounded for a month and I wasn't allowed to see David ever again! My suspension is nearly over now, but I'm dreading going back to school. My friends have told me how stupid they think I am and I've heard that David's got a new girlfriend — already! I just wish I hadn't been so stupid…"

2012's STAR SIGN SECRETS!

Whether your element is fire, earth, air or water —we reveal everything it says about you!

Turn over to find out which element *you* are! ⟶

fire △

Why you're great...

Girls born under this element are the life and soul of the party! They're radiant, captivating and enthusiastic about everything!

You'll have loads of mates because you have a positive outlook and as well as being super-popular, you're also a hit with lads, too.

You're really expressive and find it easy to give your opinions — mates are always coming to you for advice! Your confident nature means others feel comfortable around you — score!

Watch out for...

Your massive ego!

● Aries
● Leo
● Sagittarius

ARIES
March 21 — April 20

MATES — Your mates love you to pieces... but sometimes they get a bit sick of your bossy-boots attitude! Try to take a back seat sometimes and things will be swell!

DATES — Boys totally heart you, but you can sometimes give off slightly negative vibes. Try to laugh when you're having a difficult time and flash the next lad you see your killer smile — he'll go weak at the knees!

PERSONALITY TRAITS — Well, we said, you can by a lil' bossy! But deep down, you've got a heart of gold!

FASHION FIND — Fab florals are sooo you!

BEAUTY BUY — You can't live without lipbalm!

CELEB STAR SISTER — Kristen Stewart, April 9, 1990.

LEO
July 24 — August 23

MATES — Your diva-tastic attitude can sometimes embarrass your mates — and they'd rather forget the time you went mental in Pizza Hut... But they secretly love your fierce attitude! Go, girl!

DATES — You've got boys falling over each other to get close to you, but sometimes you drive them away by being so independent.

PERSONALITY TRAITS — You might only want the best for you and the people you love, but you can come across as being a lil' fussy at times — eek!

FASHION FIND — Studs unleash your inner rock chick!

BEAUTY BUY — Peep, peep, toot, toot — big hair comin' through!

CELEB STAR SISTER — Demi Lovato, August 20, 1992.

SAGITTARIUS
November 23 — December 22

MATES — You're always the life and soul of the party, but sometimes you open your mouth and drop your mates right in it...

DATES — You always go for the same guys — someone as loud and light-hearted as you! If you want a long-term boyf, though, go for someone who's a bit more down-to-earth... and who doesn't steal your limelight!

PERSONALITY TRAITS — Although you always look on the bright side of life, you're also very straight-talking.

FASHION FIND — Faux fur is totally faboosh!

BEAUTY BUY — You can't be without kohl!

CELEB STAR SISTER — Taylor Swift, December 13, 1989.

earth ▽

- Taurus
- Virgo
- Capricorn

Why you're great...

You're always thinking about others and looking out for your mates. You're reliable and hard-working, and your friends always look to you to sort out socialising with each other as you're super-organised!

You're a shoulder to cry on as you're an excellent listener and totally in tune with others.

You're supportive and down-to-earth, tending to go with your heart rather than your head in times of conflict, though you can sometimes be a little too cautious!

Watch out for...

Always playing it safe!

TAURUS
April 21 — May 21

MATES — Your mates love how down-to-earth you are... but they get a bit annoyed when you interfere with their lives — we know you love 'em but they need to make their own mistakes sometimes.

DATES — It's the total opposite with boys... you don't put yourself out there enough. Ask him out — what's the worst that could happen?

PERSONALITY TRAITS — You don't stop until you've got exactly what you want, but next time, try not to nag — ask nicely instead!

FASHION FIND — Glam glitter pumps!

BEAUTY BUY — Pretty pink nail varnish!

CELEB STAR SISTER — Miranda Cosgrove, May 14, 1993.

VIRGO
August 24 — September 23

MATES — Whether it's homework, outfits or socialising, you make sure your mates are sorted for every occasion — just make sure you're not mothering them too much!

DATES — Guys like it when you pay attention to them. Fact. But be careful not to put your crush before your mates.

PERSONALITY TRAITS — You're a total perfectionist — if a hair's out of place, you go gaga! Try to chill out, though — stressing over the little things will make you miss the bigger picture!

FASHION FIND — Cute mittens float your boat!

BEAUTY BUY — Peachy shades of blusher = ❤!

CELEB STAR SISTER — Alexandra Burke, August 25, 1988.

CAPRICORN
December 23 — January 20

MATES — Your mates sometimes think you're too serious, so show them you can let your hair down more than once in a while!

DATES — You might occasionally show your fun side to your mates, but the guy you like never gets to see it — make him laugh and you'll make him yours!

PERSONALITY TRAITS — Your motto is 'In it to win it' and you totally are! You always put in 110% effort, but remember not to be too hard on yourself if you don't meet your expectations!

FASHION FIND — Wedge shoe boots = yummy!

BEAUTY BUY — Shimmering metallic nail varnish FTW!

CELEB STAR SISTER — Frankie Sandford, January 14, 1989.

air △

Why you're great...

Miss Chatterbox is your middle name! You could talk for Britain and your bubbly, cheerful nature makes you one popular girl!

Although you're known to be a bit of a loudmouth, you have a thoughtful and caring side, and nothing can come between you and your mates.

You're intelligent and inventive and are great at speaking to all kinds of people. You're patient and kind and always have time for others — and they're always talking about how great you are!

Watch out for...

Being too much of a daydreamer!

GEMINI
May 22 — June 21

MATES — You prefer to take a back seat and let your mates take control — but they sometimes think you're being a lil' lazy! Oops!

DATES — You always seem to attract the wrong sort. Have a bit more self-belief and you'll soon be attracting boys like moths to a flame!

PERSONALITY TRAITS — You're a little too cautious sometimes — let your hair down and be brave!

FASHION FIND — Lace detail dresses!

BEAUTY BUY — Lash-lengthening mascara!

CELEB STAR SISTER — Mollie King, June 4, 1987.

LIBRA
September 24 — October 23

MATES — You know your bezzies inside-out and although it shows you love 'em, you know what makes them tick!

DATES — You're popular with boys because of your tomboyish streak... but be a lil' more girlie if you want them to see you as more than a mate!

PERSONALITY TRAITS — You're kind-hearted and sweet, but you can be a little sneaky — you don't have to make everything a drama to get attention!

FASHION FIND — Chunky knitted scarves!

BEAUTY BUY — Bright matte lipstick!

CELEB STAR SISTER — Nicola Roberts, October 5, 1985.

AQUARIUS
January 21 — February 19

MATES — You love spending time with your mates, but it's not cool when they begin to doze off because you're talking too much!

DATES — You know all the hottest guys, and you can tell they like you... but you're actually kinda shy! Fake it to make it, we say!

PERSONALITY TRAITS — You're a total gossip, and although you *try* to only use your motormouth for good, you can't help but spill all the goss — good or bad. Woopsy!

FASHION FIND — Gorge gold jewellery!

BEAUTY BUY — Shimmery grey eyeshadow!

CELEB STAR SISTER — Emma Roberts, February 10, 1991.

water ▽

● Cancer
● Scorpio
● Pisces

Why you're great...

You can be quite quiet and sometimes a little bit sensitive. You don't like to rock the boat, so you tend to let others lead the way and provide support instead.

You're naturally funny and quick-witted and always have your mates in stitches. You're a hard worker, but you love nothing more than partying with your bezzies, which is great as they love nothing more than spending time with you!

People look to you to provide them with comfort when times are bad, but also to keep the peace when times are good!

Watch out for...

Taking things too personally!

CANCER
June 22 — July 23

MATES — Your mates think you're great, but they never know how to take the things you say — don't be so sarcastic!

DATES — You think that boys never fancy you, but that's just not true! Put your happy face on and show them how great you are!

PERSONALITY TRAITS — Crikey, you're a right moody miss sometimes — we know it's only because you get so passionate about things, though!

FASHION FIND — Cute print dresses!

BEAUTY BUY — Super-hold hairspray!

CELEB STAR SISTER — Cheryl Cole, June 30, 1983.

SCORPIO
October 24 — November 22

MATES — Your mates love your laid-back attitude and sensitive nature, but they're always on edge in case you blow a fuse... eek!

DATES — Like the Katy Perry song, you're hot and cold. Stop playing boys and you'll soon get a boyfriend — simples!

PERSONALITY TRAITS — Ooh, you've got a right sting in your tail sometimes! You can be nice as pie, but if someone gets on your bad side... let's just say you don't hold back!

FASHION FIND — Bling heels!

BEAUTY BUY — Sweet-smelling perfume!

CELEB STAR SISTER — Katy Perry, October 25, 1984.

PISCES
February 20 — March 20

MATES — You've always got your mates backs, but don't let life become a competition between you!

DATES — Boys love how friendly you are towards them, but remember to be a bit mysterious... they don't need to know everything about you within five seconds of meeting!

PERSONALITY TRAITS — You're naturally talented and you love being right! Just try not to rub it in everyone's face when you're top of the class *again*...

FASHION FIND — Super-tight skinny jeans!

BEAUTY BUY — Lush liquid eyeliner!

CELEB STAR SISTER — Rihanna, February 20, 1988.

"MY RUSSIAN ACCENT STILL DRIVES ME MAD!"

LYDIA THOMPSON'S STORY STRUCK A CHORD WHEN IT WAS FEATURED IN shout **LAST YEAR — WE FOUND OUT WHAT'S HAPPENED TO HER SINCE…**

Have you ever put on a funny accent to make a friend laugh? Or what about putting on a funny voice when you do an impression of someone? That's what everyone thought I was doing when I started speaking in a Russian accent — and when I tried to tell them I wasn't faking it, they didn't believe me!

"Everyone thought I was faking it!"

"It all started when I was in a car crash. I don't remember much of what happened before the accident, and after it, I was in a coma for just over a month! When I came round from the coma, although I was weak and confused, I was able to communicate.

"When I first started speaking, Mum thought I was pronouncing my words strangely because I had an oxygen mask on, but as I started to recover, I still couldn't say words like I used to — instead of my usual accent, I sounded Russian!

"I couldn't speak normally!"

"At first my mum tried to encourage me to speak normally, but when it became clear that, no matter how hard I tried, I couldn't, she asked the doctors what could be happening to me. They said they'd never seen anything like it, and referred me to a speech therapist who would try to help me regain my speech.

"During my first appointment with the speech therapist, I was asked to read loads of words from a sheet whilst she took notes. The speech therapist admitted that she wasn't quite sure what was wrong with me, but suggested

that what I was showing signs of was Foreign Accent Syndrome (FAS) — a condition where, due to a head injury, someone can start speaking in a totally random accent!

"The speech therapist told me she'd never actually seen a case of the disorder, but that she'd speak to colleagues who had.

"However, it sounded totally like what was happening to me — I knew I couldn't help speaking strangely, and the bump on the head that caused my coma could be the one that caused problems with my speech.

"When the speech therapist came back with more information about the disorder, she concluded that I really did have the condition, and the consultant at the hospital agreed that that was what my symptoms seemed to show.

Lydia feels FAS has changed her life.

"Because FAS affects the part of the brain that controls speech, I can't actually control how my words come out — and because there have only been around 50 cases in the world, it's really difficult for doctors to know how to treat it. In fact, they're not even sure if there's a cure!

"Apparently, no-one who's ever had the condition has gone back to speaking in their normal accent, but I went to a speech therapist for a while in the hope that I'd be able to train myself to speak normally.

"I thought that since actors teach themselves to speak in foreign accents all the time, I'd be able to teach myself to do the same with my voice.

"It was really hard going back to school with the disorder. Although all my friends knew what had happened to me, and all my teachers had been told, some of my classmates laughed at me whenever I spoke.

"I also had to deal with a couple of totally cringey situations where supply teachers told me off for speaking in such a strange accent…!

"My friends have been really supportive, though, and they always help when I have to explain about my condition.

"People always think I'm putting it on!"

"The worst thing about having FAS is definitely people thinking you're putting it on… Imagine someone looking at you strangely or asking you to repeat something a million times when you do something as simple as order a McDonald's, or ask for a train ticket!

"Loads of people also think I've become fluent in Russian, so it can be embarrassing trying to convince someone that although, yes, I have a Russian accent, no, I can't actually speak the language!

"I'm used to suffering from it now!"

"There's still no cure for FAS, but since I last spoke to *Shout*, I've been coping with it a lot better.

"Now that I'm more used to suffering from FAS, I'm finding it easier to talk about it to people… most people at my school know I have it now, anyway — so I'm finding, as time goes on, that I don't have to explain myself so much!

"I stopped seeing my speech therapist as trying to go back to my normal accent just left me feeling tired and confused – I now just let my Russian accent take hold!

"I still hope that someone will come up with a cure for it as losing my voice has, sometimes, made me feel like I'm losing my identity, but if not, I guess having FAS has helped make me who I am today…"

What's Your DREAM DENIM?

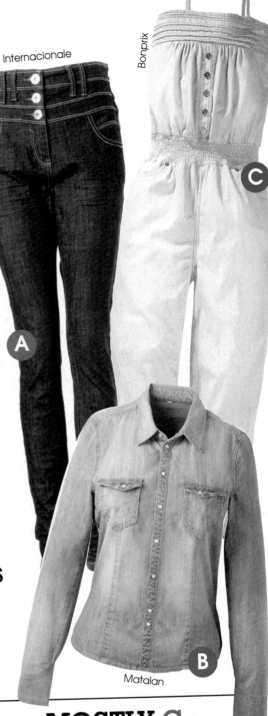

Internacionale

Bonprix

C

A

Matalan

B

DON'T BUY ANYTHING TILL YOU'VE READ THIS!

1. WHO'S STYLE DO YOU MOST ADMIRE?

A) Katy Perry.
B) Vanessa Hudgens.
C) Rihanna.

2. WHAT'S YOUR FAVOURITE ACCESSORY?

A) A cute belt.
B) A funky necklace.
C) A bright scarf.

3. THE SHOE STYLE YOU TEND TO WEAR MOST IS…

A) Plimsoll-style trainers.
B) Cute flat pumps.
C) Anything with a heel!

4. YOUR STYLE IS MAINLY…

A) Cute but casual.
B) Boho and on-trend.
C) Edgy but glam.

5. WHICH OF THESE IS YOUR BEST FEATURE?

A) Legs.
B) Tummy.
C) Arms.

MOSTLY As — SKINNY JEANS

You look great in anything which shows off your legs, so a pair of always-in-style skinny jeans is the perfect addition to your wardrobe! Wear with a white tank top and some funky trainers to be totally on-trend!

MOSTLY Bs — DENIM SHIRT

You love the boho look that the L.A. girls are rocking and a loose denim shirt is ideal for this style! Wear it open, with a plain top underneath and a big statement necklace for optimum effect!

MOSTLY Cs — DENIM JUMPSUIT

You love quirky trends and a denim jumpsuit will look great all year round! Add some cute gold jewellery and a bright belt to really stand out from the crowd, and throw a cardi over it when it gets cold!

shout ♥s YUMMY BOYS!

COULD THESE LADS BE ANY DREAMIER?!

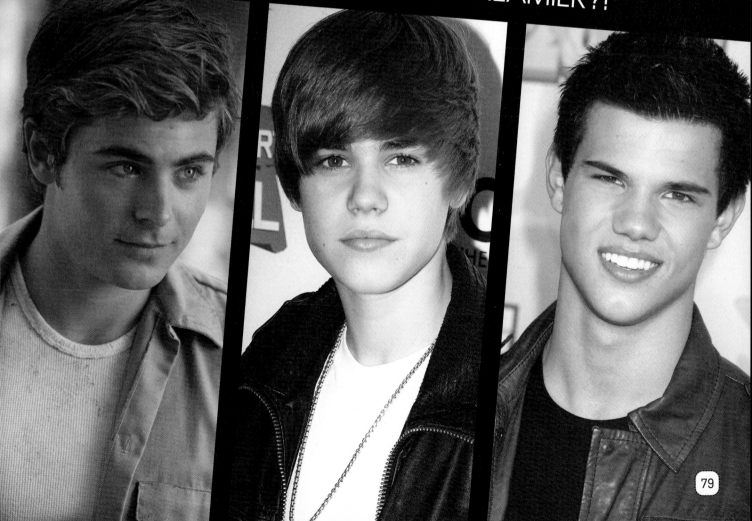

shout
TAYLOR LAUTNER

shout
ZAC EFRON

shout
IAN SOMERHALDER

ACADE
TS

CORY MONTIETH

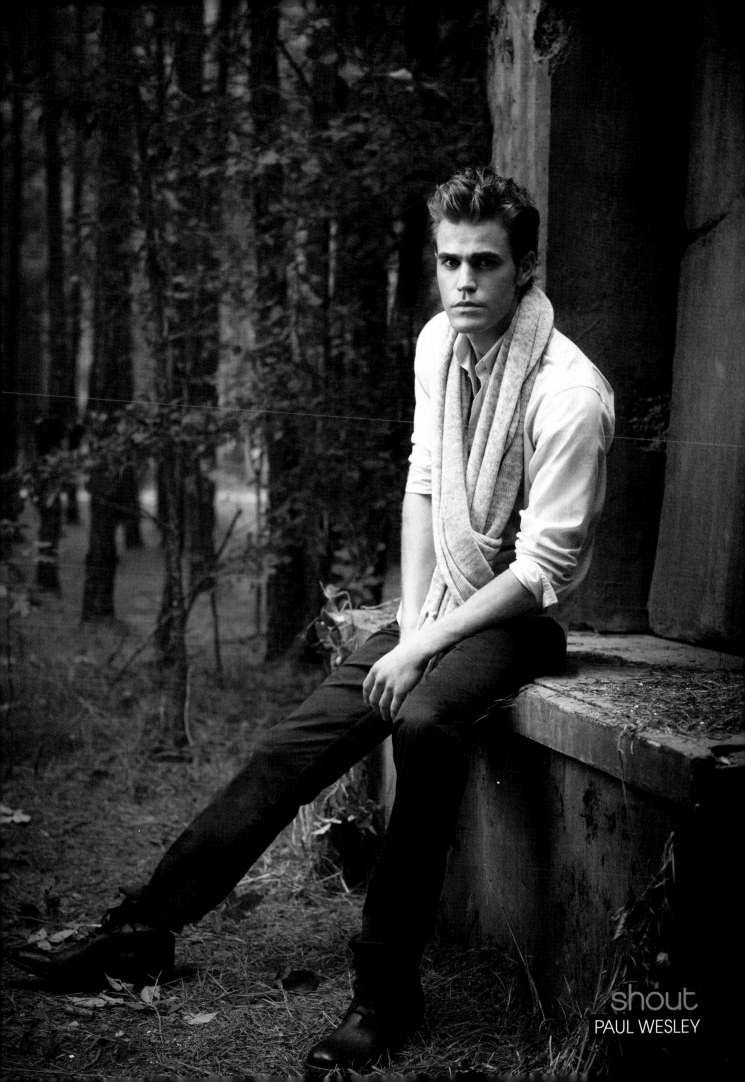

shout
PAUL WESLEY

Leighton **brightens up her winter outfit with zingy lemon and green pieces!**

Green

Urban Outfitters.

Idol at New Look.

Idol at New Look.

Alwear.

Get The Look:
Celeb

Navy

Internacionale.

Jane Norman.

Matalan.

George at ASDA.

Kim Kardashian's **blue coat gives her a retro look!**

88

Purple

Freemans.

Demi's purple dress looks great with her lighter hair!

Apricot.

Corsage, Primark.

New Look.

Colour!

Red

Frankie looks fab in this super-chic dress!

Max C.

Superlooks.com.

Apricot.

Matalan.

STOCKISTS:
Apricot www.apricotonline.co.uk
Alwear www.awear.com
Freemans www.freemans.com
Max C www.maxclondon.com
Urban Outfitters www.urbanoutfitters.co.uk
Remember, you must be over 18 to order from a catalogue,
but an older relative can order on your behalf.

the *ultimate* girls' night in!

Impress your mates with our ultimate sleepover tips!

get foodie fabulous!

OK, so snacks are obviously a key part but buying all those sweet treats can get more than a little expensive… Here's our top sleepover snacks that taste great, but won't eat into your pennies!

Cheese-on-toast Pizza

■ Toast a slice of bread on one side under the grill. Flip it over and spread with tomato purée.
■ Scatter over your fave pizza toppings — try ham, chicken, mushrooms, sweetcorn, olives or peppers — then cover with grated cheese and grill until the cheese has melted.

Always check with the 'rents that it's OK to cook! Mad Mum and Dad = ultimate sleepover cringe!

Strawberry Smoothie

■ Pour one cup of fresh orange juice, two cups of strawberry yoghurt, two cups of ice cubes and two cups of fresh strawberries into a blender and whizz up. Pour into glasses and serve!
TIP: If you're feeling flash, decorate using whipped cream and sliced strawberries or raspberries!

Microwave Brownies

■ Place four tablespoons of plain flour, one tablespoon of sugar, four tablespoons of cocoa powder, three tablespoons of water and three tablespoons of vegetable oil into a bowl with a pinch of baking powder and mix well.
■ Pour the mixture in to a microwaveable mug and cook in the microwave for about one minute (850 watt microwave), keeping an eye on it in case it bubbles over the top of the mug.
■ Remove from the microwave carefully (it'll be really hot!), leave to cool for a few minutes, then eat with ice cream!

For an extra chocolatey hit, mix in some chocolate chips! Yum!

be a pampering perfectionist!

We love getting gorgeous with the help of our mates, but we don't rate shelling out for beauty products we could make for free at home!

Sugar-sweet Lip Scrub

■ Mix up one teaspoon of honey, one teaspoon of sugar and a little bit of Vaseline. Apply to your lips and rub in gently.

■ Rinse off to reveal super-smooth, kissable lips! Mwah!

Don't like honey? Use olive oil instead!

Fabulous Facemask

■ Add one teaspoon of porridge oats to three tablespoons of honey and rub gently in to your face, avoiding your eyes.

■ Rinse off after five to ten minutes for soft, smooth, glowing skin!

For extra exfoliation, add three teaspoons of sugar to the mix!

Cheap As Chips Hand Cream!

■ Before you get your bezzie to give you a manicure, get her to rub some Vaseline in to your hands and nails, letting it soak in completely. Conditioned nails and super-soft skin, here we come!

Make sure you wash off any excess Vaseline before painting your nails!

*If you're allergic to any of the ingredients in our beauty or snack recipes, please do not attempt to make them.

shout's top ten sleepover movies!

Instead of shelling out to rent the latest film or buy it on DVD, have a classic movie marathon with our top ten favourites...

1. *High School Musical*
2. *Mean Girls*
3. *Monsters Inc*
4. *Camp Rock*
5. *Hairspray*
6. *Harry Potter*
7. *Shrek*
8. *Twilight*
9. *17 Again*
10. *Friends* (OK, it's not a film, but it's still a classic!)

You'll never get bored of drooling over Zac!

Are you team Edward or team Jacob?!

the BFF quiz!

Now it's time to see how well you and your mates know each other!

Make sure you've all got a pen and a piece of paper, and answer the following questions about one another.

There'll be loads of laughter when you reveal each others' answers, trust us!

■ **WHO WAS YOUR MATE'S FIRST CRUSH?**

■ **WHAT'S HER MOST EMBARRASSING MOMENT?**

■ **WHAT'S HER SECRET TALENT?**

■ **WHAT'S YOUR FRIEND'S FAVE FILM?**

■ **IF SHE COULD DATE ANY CELEB, WHO WOULD IT BE?**

■ **WOULD SHE RATHER HANG OUT WITH RIHANNA OR KATY PERRY?**

■ **WHAT'S HER FAVE BIT OF shout?**

■ **HAS SHE EVER HAD A BEAUTY DISASTER?**

boredom busters!

Here are our fave things to do when we've got our girlies round...

Makeover Mayhem!

Get everyone to bring over as much make-up as they can carry, dig out all your old issues of *Shout* and follow our Beauty Ed's tips!

Or why not check out YouTube for make-up tutorials if you need a little more guidance… there are some great ideas for nail art online!

Get the look!

Why not give one of your mates a celeb-inspired makeover? Here's a step-by-step guide to Katy Perry's look!

■ After gently cleansing and moisturising your mate's skin (make sure you use products suitable for her), apply foundation or tinted moisturise to her face, blending carefully.

■ Use a small brush to apply a shimmery gold eyeshadow to her lids, and just below the lash line too. Finish off her eyes with lengthening mascara.

■ Apply a pale pink lipgloss to your BFF's lips — one with a bit of shine is perfect!

■ Finish off the look by using a big brush to sweep a rosy pink blusher over the apples of her cheeks. Voila!

Play Some Choons!

Tell each of your mates to bring along a playlist on their iPod — one can make a fun chart playlist, another a cheese-tastic one, plus include a chillout mix for when you're all pampering and preening!

You'll have all your fave songs ready to put on at the press of a button and there won't be arguments over who's got control of the stereo!

Get The Goss!

There's nothing better than a good old gossip with your mates, right? OK, so you guys talk all the time, but sleepovers are a great excuse to get to know your bezzies even better — what's the best holiday they've ever been on? Who's their embarrassing celeb crush? If they had to choose between Justin Bieber and Zac Efron, who would it be? Prepare for giggles galore!